MW01065117

Sense of Smell

Carey Molter

Published by SandCastle™, an imprint of ABDO Publishing Company, 4940 Viking Drive, Edina, Minnesota 55435.

Printed in the United States.

Photo credits: Comstock, Corbis Images, Eyewire Images, PictureQuest, Stockbyte

Library of Congress Cataloging-in-Publication Data

Molter, Carey, 1973-
    Sense of smell / Carey Molter.
        p. cm. -- (The senses)
    Includes index.
    ISBN 1-57765-628-8
    1. Smell--Juvenile literature. [1. Smell. 2. Senses and sensation.] I. Title.

    QP458 .M645 2001
    612.8'6--dc21

                                                2001022905

The SandCastle concept, content, and reading method have been reviewed and approved by a national advisory board including literacy specialists, librarians, elementary school teachers, early childhood education professionals, and parents.

Let Us Know

After reading the book, SandCastle would like you to tell us your stories about reading. What is your favorite page? Was there something hard that you needed help with? Share the ups and downs of learning to read. We want to hear from you! To get posted on the Abdo Publishing Company Web site, send us email at:

sandcastle@abdopub.com

About SandCastle™

Nonfiction books for the beginning reader

- Basic concepts of phonics are incorporated with integrated language methods of reading instruction. Most words are short, and phrases, letter sounds, and word sounds are repeated.

- Readability is determined by the number of words in each sentence, the number of characters in each word, and word lists based on curriculum frameworks.

- Full-color photography reinforces word meanings and concepts.

- "Words I Can Read" list at the end of each book teaches basic elements of grammar, helps the reader recognize the words in the text, and builds vocabulary.

- Reading levels are indicated by the number of flags on the castle.

Look for more SandCastle books in these three reading levels:

Level 1 (one flag)	**Level 2** (two flags)	**Level 3** (three flags)

Grades Pre-K to K 5 or fewer words per page	**Grades K to 1** 5 to 10 words per page	**Grades 1 to 2** 10 to 15 words per page

Our senses tell us what
is going on around us.

Smell is one of our five senses.

Our noses tells us what something smells like.

Sally takes a bath to
smell fresh and clean.

Onions have a strong smell.

They make my eyes water.

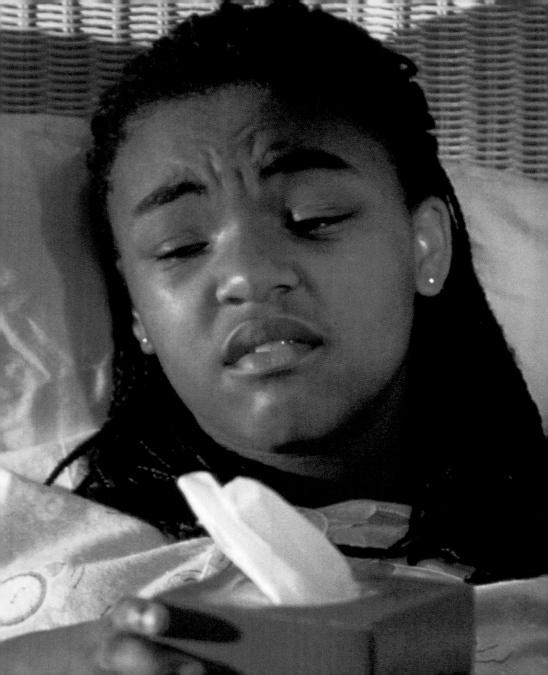

When Teena has a cold
she cannot smell
anything.

Some fish have a stinky smell.

This fish smells bad.

Paula smells the flower.

It smells like perfume.

Nora and her mother
bake cookies.

How do you think
that smells?

Words I Can Read

Nouns

A noun is a person, place, or thing

bath (BATH) p. 11
cold (KOHLD) p. 15
fish (FISH) p. 17
flower (FLOU-ur) p. 19
mother
  (MUHTH-ur) p. 21

perfume
  (PUR-fyoom) p. 19
smell (SMEL) pp. 7, 13, 17

Plural Nouns

A plural noun is more than one person, place, or thing

cookies (KUK-eez) p. 21
eyes (EYEZ) p. 13
fish (FISH) p. 17
noses (NOHZ-EZ) p. 9

onions (UHN-yuhnz) p. 13
senses
  (SENSS-ez) pp. 5, 7

Proper Nouns

A proper noun is the name of a person, place, or thing

Nora (NOR-uh) p. 21
Paula (PAW-luh) p. 19

Sally (SAL-ee) p. 11
Teena (TEE-nuh) p. 15

Verbs

A verb is an action or being word

are (AR) p. 21

baking (BAYK-ing) p. 21

cannot (KAN-ot) p. 15

do (DOO) p. 21

going (GOH-ing) p. 5

has (HAZ) p. 15

have (HAV) pp. 13, 17

is (IZ) pp. 5, 7

make (MAKE) p. 13

smell (SMEL) pp. 11, 15

smells (SMELZ)
   pp. 9, 15, 17, 19, 21

takes (TAYKSS) p. 11

tell (TEL) p. 5

think (THINGK) p. 21

water (WAW-tur) p. 13

Adjectives

An adjective describes something

bad (BAD) p. 17

clean (KLEEN) p. 11

five (FIVE) p. 7

fresh (FRESH) p. 11

her (HUR) p. 21

my (MYE) p. 13

one (WUHN) p. 7

some (SUHM) p. 17

stinky (STINGK-ee) p. 17

strong (STRONG) p. 13

this (THISS) p. 17

More About the Sense of Smell
Match the Words to their Pictures

smoky

sniff

smelly

nostril

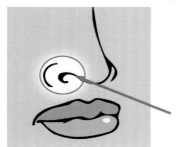